# I went, I was lost, I was found, I experienced



Miriam Itzkowitz

BookLeaf Publishing

I went, I was lost, I was found, I experienced


Presentation by *BookLeaf Publishing*

Web: www.bookleafpub.com

E-mail: info@bookleafpub.com

ISBN: 9789357619967

First edition 2022

# DEDICATION

*To my loving grandparents, Bubbe and Zayde,*
*and Grandma and Grandpa.*

# ACKNOWLEDGEMENT

I would like to acknowledge my incredible family, friends, and mentors for always believing in me and allowing me to pursue my dreams and achieve my goals, namely my parents, Seth and Suzie, who have consistently encouraged me, and my grandparents, Ann (Bubbe) and Marty (Zayde), and Paul (Grandpa) and Annette (Grandma), who have always supported me in all my unusual and ambitious endeavours. I would also like to acknowledge my (not so) little brother, Alexander, for always being there for me, annoying me, and inspiring me every day. I love you all. From the bottom of my heart: thank you.

# PREFACE

This is a collection of works I have written throughout my teenage years, reflecting on my relationship with my mental health, my Jewish identity and connection to Israel, and the world around me. There have been minimal edits in order to maintain the raw emotion from the moments these pieces were written.

As I emerge from adolescence and transition into difficult-to-navigate adulthood, I hope to use this book as a reminder and indicator of my growth and progress from teenager to young woman. I hope this book serves as an inspiration to young people everywhere, especially young Jews, young girls, and young people struggling with their mental health, acknowledging their struggles, and letting them know that their experiences are valid and important, and deserve to be heard and told.

The title comes from one of my pieces of writing, which uses Hebrew phrases and words, some from the Torah, which I felt shaped my first time in Israel, as well as how I now go about every aspect of my life. The words are:

“Lech Lecha” (go forth), “Ayekah?” (where are you?), “Hineni” (I am here), and “Chavayah” (experience). These four phrases/words each shape how I perceive the goings on in my life: “go forth” - try something new, step outside your comfort zone, “where are you?” - what is my starting point?, “I am here” - this is my progress, how far I've come, and “experience” - the conclusion and reflection on the event. I have found this to be incredibly meaningful in navigating the big, scary world around me, anticipating a fully adult life ahead, and it has also proven useful in my writing.

# Contents

# My Head's in the Clouds

Look at me up here
In the clouds
The magical islands floating above pools of blue
Hundreds and hundreds of them
Each with their own unique kinks and quirks
I hop from one to the next
Each cosy and warm
Filling my heart with pure joy

The first one lets me look at the world below
Stupid, absent-minded beings scurrying along
Oblivious to the beauty surrounding them
The beauty above them
The tall trees dancing in the wind
The flowers at their fullest bloom
Even the tiny creatures trying to make it down in that crazy world
I say goodbye to the cloud
I know I will never see him again, for he will be no more

The second one lets me look into the infinite universe
He shows me every star
Their beauty is beguiling

They shine
They twinkle
They're truly alluring
I thank the cloud
“They're dead” he says
I sink
I drown in sorrow
These glowing lights are dead?
“But their beauty still shines for eternity”
And then I see the stars
Even if I couldn't see them when they were still alive, I can see them now
I can see what incredible lives they led
I say goodbye to the cloud
I know I will never see him again, for he will be no more

The third cloud lets me rest in his warmth
I snuggle into the blanket of vapour
I enter, my mind prepared for exploration
I meet the villagers in this cloud
Each of them as nice as can be
Each of us in complete and utter euphoria
I awake in peace
I say goodbye to the cloud
I know I will never see him again, for he will be no more

Just as I'm about to return home, I see a green cloud
Intrigued, I get closer
He looks distressed
He's spitting out green rain
He's crying
He's in pain
I rush over to comfort him
“Stay back!”, he screams
I tell him I want to help
He tells me there's nothing I can do
I ask him what happened
He tells me about the absent-minded beings
How they don't take time to appreciate their surroundings the way I do
How they're selfish and rushing through life too quickly
Rather than helping or paying attention to others
So even though they're taking care of themselves, trying to make sure they’re ok
They don’t care about anything else
Everything else is suffering badly
I promise him I will try and make a change
I say goodbye to the cloud
I know I will never see him again, for he will be no more

And I will make a change

# The Scapegoat

Why do people hate me?
Blame me for all the world's problems?
Because apparently I'm at fault for other people's lack of success
Apparently I only care about my friends and family
And apparently I'm more loyal to a country of which I'm not citizen

Apparently I'm wealthy
If I donate money, apparently it's to show my wealth
If I keep it, apparently it's because I'm miserly
Why can't I win?
Why can't I just be a kind person who wants to help this world?
Why is every action of mine dictated by my culture?

It's because people are angry
At others' successes
They feel threatened
That a group so small
Can thrive and flourish
Despite the hells we've been through
The truth is we act just like anyone else would

But because we're “different” we're the ones
who have to suffer from the excessive
judgement
We're the ones who get called names
Just for acting like anyone else
We're the ones who are labelled “murderers”
Despite the fact that we're the victims
We are forever cursed with hate

The truth is that people hate themselves
They hate how they act
They notice others who act like them
And then pin that action on the minute group
who is doing the same thing as everyone else
That's how messed up our world is
Pointing to innocent scapegoats
Who have experienced this torment
Without knowing why

Why do you do it?
Why do you hurt us?
What have I -
What have *we* ever done to you as a people?
And no, we are not all cheats
Not all of us are greedy
Not all of us are rich
Not all of us are successful
But we're all a people
We're all The Scapegoat

# The Dream is Just a Dream

The dream was beautiful
Magical in fact
She felt like the most special girl in the entire world
His smiling eyes gazed at her with such joy
He sat level at her standing
Not wanting her to go
His soft, comforting voice letting her know

At another point, he towered over her
Grabbing her arm
Don't go, he'd sweetly whisper
Never, she assured

She imagined their happy life together
Formals, graduations, dinners
A wedding
Children
Growing old together
Sleeping together for all eternity
By each other's sides in blissful peace

But the dream is just a dream
It's broken

It’s flawed
It’s fake

She tells him of her wonderful dream
Accidentally, he crushes it
Destroys it with his words
His mighty words
His powerful words
His honest words

The dream crumbles into a nightmare
And hits her with reality
As though she’s awoken from a daze
She feels numb
She has been living a lie
Nothing will change, he tells her
He still loves her the same

But it’s too late
The damage has been done
She is broken
Confused
Sad

Her fictitious dreams mean nothing to reality
Her little island of imagination and pure joy
deemed fake by him
Reality tries his best to be kind

But harshly reminds her that she actually lives in his world
Where everything is just so
Reality refuses to open his mind up
He's decided that things are just the way they are
They won't ever change
And he won't even indulge slightly in her dreams
Ever.

She takes a breath
And sulkily and reluctantly joins reality
Where he nor she will ever be truly happy

# Where Nature Dies

Silence.
Rows of five.
We marched
Into the forest
In broad daylight
No words could be spoken

The birds chirped loudly as we held on - to the one thing that differentiated us from the others; our identity. They couldn't relate and they won't ever.

Were we meant to be wearing our identity with pride? It was too difficult. What is the point in being proud when the death of thousands is imminent? Our pride is futile.

In our rows of five, we stopped at the pit. The deep pit filled to the top with bodies.

Our own bodies filled with fear and upset, overwhelmed. Helpless.

We left the forest - powerless. But we were safe. And still proud. Proud to be Jews. Proud to be alive. Proud to carry on the legacy of these anonymous martyrs.

# Invalidity

A play about a cheat was written for her
To offend her
Because she's Jewish
He was bullied
And comments were made about money
Because he's Jewish
Someone drew swastikas on her desk
And pretended to be her friend
Because she's Jewish
Someone spread lies
And told everyone that I have a big hook nose
Because I'm Jewish

Yet, I feel as though my experiences are incomparable
To the experiences of those whose seem worse and more severe than my own
And to those of the people who died in the Holocaust
My anti-Semitic experiences are nothing

People secluded and isolated them
And murdered them
Because they were Jewish

# My Messy Mind

Oh, my messy mind
What a grave pain in the neck
You are annoying

I have disorders
Oh, way too many to count
They pain me greatly

They're complicated
Controlling my life, they are
This is way too much

My anxiety
Social and generalised
Ah! this is scary

Do they all hate me?
Will the world start to explode?
Monster under bed?

Inconvenience.
At times I'm scared to go out
Oh, this is too much!

Oh, ADHD
Unfocused and distracted
I can't concentrate

It makes my mind loud
Oh look over there - a bug!
What was I saying?

Oh yes, sometimes I...
... sorry, I was daydreaming!
I get lost in thou-

Stupid OCD
With you I cannot function
I'm stuck in the mud

Can't do this until
I do that, can't do that un-
til I finish this

Oh, OCPD
Yay! Yippee! A disordered
personality

Perfectionism
It's so called. Bit ironic...
I can't do a thing

Ripping out pages
of working until it's right
So time consuming!

Procrastination
My best friend; just one more vid
Need an extension

Assignments pile up
Dear professor please help me
My brain's a li'l shit

I swear I've studied
And paid attention in class
I just love YouTube

Panic attacks and
starting all over again
Reorganising

This ain't in order
This reading has lots of words
I am giving up

I've a messy mind
Yes, it's painful to admit
Alas, it is mine

# Parallely Different

Two teenagers
Same age
Same interests
Practically the same lives
But completely different

Both are stressed
One because they don't know which university to apply to
The other, because they don't know which army position to apply for

Both are depressed
One because they were dumped by their significant other
The other, because their older sibling was just killed in action

Both are upset
One because their dream school rejected them
The other, because they were selected for combat instead of their first preference because they are "too healthy"

Both are nervous
One because tomorrow is their first day of college
The other, because tomorrow is their first day of army service

Two teenagers
Same age
Same interests
Practically the same lives
But now about to be completely different

# I went, I was lost, I was found, I experienced

לך לך

I was told to go, leave, on an adventure. I was told to "return" to a place I had never been because it was my duty as a Jew. But I didn't know what it meant to be a Jew. I knew the songs, traditions, prayers, but I didn't understand why it was my duty to love a place I had no physical connection to.

I arrived wide-eyed and ready to learn. I wanted to learn, no - needed to learn why, I, a Diasporan Jew, had to love this country. I already loved it. But why? I made this my mission for my adventure. Even with the little history I knew, I didn't know how to justify my love without sounding completely biased by the simple fact that "I'm Jewish", as though this was an expectation of me from the moment I was born and that was reason enough. But it wasn't.

Lech Lecha

איכה

We knew where we were but we didn't. How were we to navigate such a place of most certain complexity? So rich in history. So politically complex. We were definitely assisted in this area. We were all split into classes to explore this land to its fullest depth.

My teacher looked different to me. He too shared a love for this land. How could it be that we both shared the common love for this place, for presumably the same reasons, yet, we were so different?

This man had kind eyes. He always smiled. He was whimsical and rabbinical and musical and wise. His passion for this country was contagious. While we were all lost in this holy land, it was he who guided our way. He didn't tell us where we were. He showed us. And so we were able to discover it ourselves.

Ayekah

הנני
After five weeks of searching, I found where I was. This land was mine. Its beauty and riches and history all belong to me. Because I'm a Jew. I finally understood why this was my land. Why I should love it. How I could justify it. I knew that this place was my home. For me. Whenever I need it. It's here. And I can rightfully come. As a Jew. A Jew who loves this country. A Zionist.

I understood the history inside and out. I know why we belong here. I know why it is ours. I have no shame in being in love with this land. It has MY history. It contains the story of MY people. MY people are the majority. I feel tolerated. I feel accepted. I feel loved. This is the land we were exiled from and our ancestors kept fighting and working and fighting and working so it could be ours again. And still today people fight, so we can have our land. People lose their lives for this land.

Hineni

חוויה

My experience has been surreal. The chutzpah. The ruach. The history. The joy. The danger. The solemnity. It all makes up this land. I've prayed at the wall that was there to protect our holy site, but was destroyed due to hatred. I've rejoiced to the music that unites people everyday, encouraging smiles upon their faces. I've learnt in an outdoor classroom with the history right in front of me. I've heard gunshots and seen terrorist flags, in protest that this country, my country should exist. I've cried at the cemetery, knowing that so many people have died to bring this country into existence and preserve it, and that more will continue to follow in our fallen's footsteps. I've walked this land, just as my ancestors did, who came here, tended to it, were exiled, yet still continued to come back and tend to it some more. I've experienced this land.

And yet I still question my right to this land. I love it. I can justify it fairly. No bias. But still. I question the sacrifices made for this land's existence. Why do some people survive and others don't? Why should people die or suffer for my right to a land? I don't want to be a part of something where people are sacrifices in order to keep a land. Yet, people do. But why? Why should people be hurt, killed, murdered, slaughtered just so I can have a land? Some are willing to die for this land. Others aren't. How is this justified? How is it worth it?

How can such a beautiful land be a place of horrors and misery and inequality? How can this be my land? Yet I still love it. With all its flaws. I do. Because I've experienced the land. I've experienced Israel. I know its power. I know its vulnerability. I know Israel. I know that it’s flawed. But, I also know that I will come back and experience it all over again.

Chavayah

# Little Miss Anxious

Meet Little Miss Anxious
Little Miss Anxious is a lovely girl
She is always well-intentioned
But she has a bad habit of over-thinking everything
And getting caught in somewhat unfortunate situations more often than not

Take today, for example
Little Miss Anxious went out on a boat
She checked the weather forecast prior
Fifty percent chance of perfect weather
Fifty percent chance it will be horrible

Being her optimistic self, Little Miss Anxious decided not to bring her life jacket
What's the point?
Life jackets are bulky and are just another thing to remember
Best to alleviate herself of as much responsibility as possible in order to have a good time

Little Miss Anxious carefully, but clumsily (she is somewhat of a klutz), stumbled onto the boat, rocking it slightly as it drifted out to sea
The weather was seemingly perfect as the sun shone brightly in the sky, warming Little Miss Anxious up and reflecting happiness around her
All seemed perfect until Little Miss Anxious noticed the gentle rocking

What if?, she thought
The most dangerous thought: what if?
Little Miss Anxious has these "what if" thoughts multiple times throughout the day:
What if her friends are angry with her?
What if her outfit doesn't suit her?
What if no one loves her?
What if her crush turns out to be a serial killer supervillain who falsely confesses his love to her in an attempt to kidnap her and chop her up into little pieces and feed her to the sharks and nobody notices that she's gone?
What if he rejects her?

In this case, Little Miss Anxious' "what if" thoughts were, perhaps, a bit more rational
What if the weather changes its mind?
What if the boat becomes unsteady and the waters unsafe?
What if she drowns?

And then, as if the universe were reading her mind, the clouds invaded and conquered the bright sky, imprisoning the sun behind their dark, cold barrier
The sun tried to peer out to tell Little Miss Anxious that everything was going to be ok, that it would be back soon, but it succumbed to its captors and hid its light away from her
As the sky darkened, Little Miss Anxious became increasingly filled with “what if” thoughts:
What if she's stuck at sea?
What if she capsizes?
What if she dies?

The clouds, sensing her fears and nervousness, chuckled to themselves
She's stupid for not bringing her life jacket, and yet, she's scared, they sneered
Let's teach her a little lesson, shall we?
Then, as if habitual and executed flawlessly, the clouds started taking turns blowing Little Miss Anxious and her boat around the sea, shaking her up considerably
The gentle rocking became heavier, turning into violent sways
Little Miss Anxious shuddered
What if she doesn't make it out alive?

What if she drowns and nobody cares because it
was a dumb mistake to forget her life jacket?
What if this is all just a nightmare?

As she held on for dear life, the clouds grew
meaner
Let's drench her!, they cheered
Then, as if to prepare her for life under the sea,
they spat on her
Pellets and pellets of cloud spit drenched poor
Little Miss Anxious
What if the rain gets worse?, thought Little Miss
Anxious
The clouds, having predicted this very thought,
started crying from laughter
Oh, how naïve Little Miss Anxious was!
The tears from their laughter and their continued
blowing of her boat caused the shaking to turn
into a severe bout of seesawing, causing water
from the sea to begin to spill into Little Miss
Anxious' tiny vessel
She felt scared, helpless, afraid

Unsure of what to do, Little Miss Anxious
reverted to her usual habit
The dangerous "what if" thoughts
What if this gets worse?

What if she doesn't come out of this alive?
What if the clouds are truly out to get her?

Sensing her regret at being out at sea in such conditions, the clouds continued to have no mercy
Let's scare her some more!, they cheered
Maintaining the blowing and laughter tears, they surrounded her with spiky flashes of brightness, followed by loud cackles and shouts
Bright flash
Boo!
Another flash
Crack!
More and more and more they continued, causing Little Miss Anxious quite the panic
What if this is the end?
What if nobody cares?
What if her death is celebrated?

The clouds, finding her reactions amusing, increased everything
Blowing
Screaming
Crying
Howling
Little Miss Anxious whimpered as her boat started filling with water and sinking
There was nothing she could do to stop it

Splash!
Her boat capsized
She tried to stay up above the water, unsuccessfully though, as the waves crashed over her, pushing her under the surface
And the seas and the winds and the seaweed kept trying to pull her down
She struggled and tugged with all her might
Fighting her way out, kicking and screaming
But it was exhausting
Water seeping down her throat, into her eyes, filling her ears
Like the sun, she succumbed to nature

She awoke on the shore, her friends glaring at her with disappointment
Where were you?
We were worried!
You can't keep going on like this...
Mr Grumpy Beard raised his thick eyebrows
You should have brought your life jacket
But it's too hard!, Little Miss Anxious protested
It's bulky and heavy and too much to remember!
But it will keep you safe, he replied
We won't have to worry so much, added Little Miss Bossy Boots
But none of you guys use it, retorted Little Miss Anxious

That's because we're better at dealing with the evil clouds and the rough seas, Angsty, answered Miss Bossy Boots

You're just not as strong as the rest of us

But it's not fair, Bossy, cried Little Miss Anxious

She's right, Angsty, Mr Grumpy Beard joined in

You don't need to be embarrassed or ashamed to admit your weakness...

But everyone will judge me, Grumpy

No they won't. Lots of people wear life jackets, and one day, when you're strong enough, you won't need to wear your life jacket anymore.

Do you really think so?

I know so.

So, tomorrow, Little Miss Anxious will go back on the water in her boat, wearing her life jacket, feeling less afraid

Maybe she'll go with Mr Grumpy Beard or with Little Miss Bossy Boots

But it won't matter either way because she'll be safe with her life jacket

And who knows? Maybe one day, she won't need her life jacket anymore

# Creep Magnet

I am a creep magnet
No, seriously I am
Whenever I try to attract a gent
The result is, I must scram

I make myself look very cute
The guys all stare in awe
Then they say I'm like a child
I want to punch them in the jaw

They like me being short
They think I'm still in school
It feels really alt and edgy
And it makes them drool

I want to be seen as a woman
Despite being young and small
I should always be treated as equal
Compared to anyone at all

So if you are a man
On a conquest for a date
Make sure you make her feel special
You better not be late

But don't tell her that she's like a kid
That's not what she want to hear
She wants to attract a real man
And not creepy men, my dear

Alas, I'm still a creep magnet
I hope that it won’t last
Once I find my special one
It will all be in the past

# We've Never Truly Left

Open gates
Fresh air
With a rubbery stench
Black soil
Yellow flowers everywhere
Dead silence.

The empty barracks are filled with fear, misery, and despair
One can sense the tragedy that occurred in these dark, dark giant rooms not so long ago
The stench intensifies creating an intoxicating fixation with the people of the past
They are still here

Candles
Lights
Nets
Names
Places
Gloom
Pure dead darkness
Reflection
Misery
Silence

Cries of pain and sorrow
And still there's silence

Shoes
Piles of shoes
Stacks of shoes
Lots and lots of shoes
The only remnants of the murdered's identities
The only remains of their individuality
Before they were ruthlessly stripped of
themselves - of who they were - and slaughtered
like farm animals - no, worse than farm animals
Slaughtered as though their lives meant nothing
Slaughtered as though they were a burden or
disadvantage to the human race
Slaughtered as though they did something
detrimentally wrong
And all they had left were shoes
Just shoes
The things meant to protect our feet but provide
no protection of life
Shoes shouldn't be their legacy
And they're not

The cold air is repelled by the sunny sky as I sit
on the ground
Staring
At the yellow flower
Growing out of the black dirt

Coloured by the human ash
Which will take a thousand years to return to its original state
How ironic that such a beautiful life can come out of such terrible deaths

People.
They were people

Barracks and barracks
They eventually evolve into Satan's real lair
When you enter you already begin to feel trapped and helpless
Everything so big and you so insignificant
But now the Hell is real and true
Your previous feelings seem invalid as you see the true atrocities

Ovens
Scratches on walls
Cries for help
Beds to disembowel bodies
Drains for blood
To rob from the dead
The hurt
The victims of monsters

Monsters who turned innocent people into smithereens

Monsters who used the heat of the ovens to provide them with warmth and comfort in a sauna
Monsters who haunted the last thoughts that these victims ever had

People who had real ambitions and hopes and dreams
Burnt into dust
And used
As fertiliser

A pile of dust
A pile of loss
A pile of dirt
A pile of ash
Filled with wannabe writers, athletes, doctors, mechanics, dreamers
Now a mound of intermingled remains

No Jew can truly ever leave Majdanek
We left alive but cannot forget this place
We are forever imprisoned there; trapped
But as survivors

# Shoes

The shoes of the dead lie stacked together
That gigantic one belonged to the businessman
And that teeny-tiny one belonged to a
two-year-old girl
That shiny one belonged to the cobbler
And that fluffy one belonged to the
seventy-year-old grandmother who loved to
bake cakes
That rough one is from the teenage athlete who
wore it out over the years
And that smooth one belonged to the girl who
received it as a present for when she started
school
That black one belonged to the rabbi
And that white one belonged to the ballet dancer
That scarred one belonged to the poor orphan
boy who couldn't afford shoes because his
parents were taken away and he had to hide
And that heavy one belonged to the lawyer
They all belonged to someone
Different someones

# Annoying Dumb Horrible Demon

Annoying

All I do is try to pay attention to what's going on but I can't - it's too hard
Time and again I find myself on some random Wikipedia page to do with a point that my teacher said which reminded me of another thing which reminded me of another thing that I had to research which leads me down this weird rabbit hole and I end up reading the list of sexually active popes or watching a video on Jihadi John - the distractions are endless really
Tomorrow will be different I tell myself - I will be able to concentrate and get everything done and be on top of my work
Effort starts high but as soon as something becomes slightly difficult my brain goes walkabout to daydreaming about my perfect man - tall, dark, and handsome - with an interest in science - and me of course and then I realise that this is likely not a possible scenario and that I should set more realistic expectations for myself in my everyday life such as not getting distracted and procrastinating - oh wait - I'm doing it again

Nothing irks me more than the fact that I cannot remain focused for elongated amounts of time
The second my phone buzzes or I get an e-mail my ears prick up and eyes start to wander and even if I turn off my notifications I will get distracted by wondering if I am missing out on an important notification or if my muse has messaged me a witty response
I know how ridiculous this sounds - how can she not control herself? - but it's true - my concentration is truly an impossible achievement
Only those who possess the Annoying Dumb Horrible Demon can understand
No one else does

Dumb

Doing anything at any time of day is difficult for me
Everyone thinks I'm just slow or stupid even though I'm actually kinda smart
Frustratingly my production of work doesn't always demonstrate this even though it's true
I do get good grades but my reliance on extensions is the only thing keeping me from failing
Continuously I disappoint myself because I know I'm capable of doing better - my brain just doesn't allow me to

I am not dumb -I'm not - I just have the Annoying Dumb Horrible Demon who makes me and others at times think I am
That sucks

Horrible

Hysterically I rush to complete my assignments and work sometimes on the verge of panic
Years of living like this I revert to my usual fidgeting: shaking and scratching my thumb against my index finger and rocking back and forth and tapping
People don't always notice but when they do they sometimes yell saying that I'm being annoying and distracting - ha! if only they knew that that's what's happening to me twenty-four-seven
Every single second I think about how exhilarating and relieving it would be to stand up and walk out and run around or stretch or just have an entire hour to fidget and move my body like crazy just to get all the jitters out
Realistically this is not possible and I have to concentrate on staying as still as humanly possible so as not to be a distraction but also concentrate on what is going on around me and if people are talking what they are saying and concentrate on trying to pay attention whilst trying to maintain a poised and mature façade

At times people accuse me of looking for attention - wrong! I want no attention on me - the only attention I want is that to be able to pay which I am currently lacking

Clicking my pen is a massive stress relief - it keeps me calm and divides my focus

The Annoying Dumb Horrible Demon has some lesser known antidotes which repel his interference but often people want those antidotes repelled themselves

I dislike how fidget spinners were banned at school - believe me if I knew that the Annoying Dumb Horrible Demon was haunting me then you can bet your bottom dollar that I would have used it to get through the day - it would have been so helpful

Violent internal outbursts of self-disappointment in being unable to conform to a concentrating statue occur

It feels like a club that I'm not a part of - one for only the most skilled at freezing their loud brains and turning their focus to one thing without any struggles

Their minds are like noise-cancelling headphones

Yet I'm jealous as my mind is more like a radio with a broken antenna on full volume taking bits of information from every which way and causing me confusion and distress for which element of noise to tune in on - not an easy decision and either way it doesn't matter because the second I decide another channel will become louder and disrupt the one I'm already listening to which lures me away into a zone of distractibility

Demon

Dearest Annoying Dumb Horrible Demon,
I kindly ask you to fuck off
Sorry for being rude but I really can't take it anymore
On the one hand I love milking the benefits of Disability Services but in
Reality the amount of stress and anxiety caused by you is debilitating
Days in bed being unable to move and bouts of panic and freak-outs and thinking that I'm not good enough because you cause me to be distracted and to have a loud brain all day every day
Everyone already thinks I'm weird enough so you don't need to add another item to their probably already extensive list
Regards, A Distressed Humiliated Damsel

# HaTikvah

HaTikvah is that I can live in safety
HaTikvah is that there will be peace
HaTikvah is that I can express my views without judgement
HaTikvah is that I am accepted for who I am
HaTikvah is that my country represents EVERYBODY
HaTikvah is that everybody is treated equally in my country
HaTikvah is that my country is inclusive
HaTikvah is that everybody should be able to express their religion freely

HaTikvah was the establishment of a Jewish State
HaTikvah was for all Jews to live in safety
HaTikvah was meant to be peaceful
HaTikvah was meant to tolerate everybody
HaTikvah was meant to accept me
HaTikvah was meant to represent its citizens and treat them equally
HaTikvah was meant to be inclusive
HaTikvah was meant to show faith in a safe haven for all Jews

How far has HaTikvah really come? How much has HaTikvah really helped us?

There are still citizens in danger
There is still war
There is still intolerance and discrimination
There are still people who wouldn't consider me a Jew
There are still many underrepresented and who don't have a say
There are still many who are mistreated
There are still many who are excluded
There are still many who are uncomfortable or judged for expressing their religion freely

If this is all HaTikvah has accomplished, I don't want a part of it. It merely seems like an idealistic, utopian fantasy, painted by those who really cared and tried to pursue their collective dream. Was it really achieved though?

The Holy Land has many amazing qualities, countered by the terror that contradicts HaTikvah. I don't want HaTikvah.

I want HaTzedek, so that everyone is a free and equal citizen
I want HaOsher, so that everyone has the opportunity to smile

I want HaB'tichut, so that everyone can go
outside without fear, or without horrific
circumstances
I want HaSovlanut, so that everybody feels
accepted for being who they are
I want HaHognut, so that everybody is given a
chance
I want HaHachalah, so that we can all celebrate
each other together
I want HaYicholet Lihi'ot Atzmi, especially in
this country that is meant to also belong to me

Until these things change, I humbly dissent
HaTikvah. I want HaShalom.

# Order

Same
Dark green, red, light blue, yellow
My
Two
It
Left
The
Facebook
This
7am
Or

Spot
Light green, gold, aqua, black
Routine
Three
Must
Right
World
Gmail
Has
10am
Else

Every
Light orange, dark orange, light brown, dark brown
Is
Five
Work
Left
Will
Twitter
To
12:30pm
I

Single
Pink, purple, blue, dark blue
My
Seven
Like
Right
End
Instagram
Remain
5:30pm
Will

Day
Grey, peach, silver, white
Everything
Eleven
Clockwork
Left
Otherwise
YouTube
Perfect
6pm
Die

# 70 Thousand

The cemetery is full of graves. Hundreds and thousands of them. They died peacefully, well, most of them. Except for those who were brutally murdered. Some in graves, most in pits. Three big pits. Three big pits filled with seventy thousand bodies respectively.

Their deaths were not peaceful. They were a joke. Why weren't they deserving of proper burials? Because they were Jews in the wrong place at the wrong time. That doesn't seem fair. Seventy thousand plus seventy thousand plus seventy thousand Jews could not all have been in the wrong place at the wrong time. That excuse is lame. Seventy thousand plus seventy thousand plus seventy thousand Jews could not have done anything to deserve such a terrible fate and seventy thousand plus seventy thousand plus seventy thousand Jews deserve a proper burial. To be acknowledged. Because they are true martyrs. Jewish martyrs who deserve much much more than what they got - before and after death. Seventy thousand plus seventy thousand plus seventy thousand names and faces will forever be forgotten. But their legacy won't be. They died for us.

# Perfect

I am perfect

Wait, let me start again

I am perfect
I am flawless
Everyone wants to be me
I get good grades
I'm pretty
I'm nice
I'm smart
I have amazing friends
People are amazed at my success and practically grovel at my feet
And it's so easy to be like me

No, it sounds bad, let me start again again

I am perfect
I am flawless
Everyone wants to be me
I get good grades
I'm pretty
I'm nice
I'm smart

I have amazing friends
People are amazed at my success and practically grovel at my feet
And it's so easy to be like me
I'm also super modest and open and honest and humble

No! This is too difficult, I need to start again...

I am perfect
I am flawless
Everyone wants to be me
I get good grades
I'm pretty
I'm nice
I'm smart
I have amazing friends
People are amazed at my success and practically grovel at my feet
And it's so easy to be like me
I'm also super modest and open and honest and humble
I have so many talents
I can sing
I can write
I can speak multiple languages
My spelling skills? On point

I have great, big, different ideas, and if people knew what was good for them, they'd agree with me

Ughh, no. This is too hard. I give up.

The truth is, I'm not perfect
No matter how hard I try
I know that no one is perfect, but I still strive for perfection in everything I do
I'm just not always successful in doing so
But I try over and over and over to get it right
Mistake in my working? Rip out the page or rub it out and start all over again
Outfit looks bad? Yank everything out of my closet until I find the perfect ensemble

I am not flawless
I can't get through a single day without picking myself apart
Too many pimples
Too much eczema
Too much hair
Boobs too big
Butt too big
Hips too wide
Not fit enough
Hair too curly
Hair too knotty

Tan faded too much - you're starting to look white!

No one wants to be me
The pressure I put myself under every day
The constant panic I feel
No one would wish this upon their worst enemy, let alone themselves

I do get good grades
But I only do so because I freak myself out enough to make my work practically perfect
My paper wastage from printing is astonishing
Needing to rewrite everything perfectly
One simple mistake and my world crumbles
It has to be perfect

I'm not pretty
Well, I'm not ugly
I don't actually know
Some days I put in zero effort and walk around in my pyjamas (which are really just a giant shirt and a hoodie)
Other days, I pamper myself, make sure my hair looks nice, and even do my make-up if I want to feel really special
Those are the only times I'm called pretty
Otherwise, I'm just a slob

I'm not nice
I mean, I usually am
But sometimes I can be such a bitch
I try to be nice to everyone
But sometimes people just really piss me off
Say the wrong thing
Just do something annoying
Upset me
And then I will either have a go at them if I'm feeling comfortable and confident
Or I'll be a sly little twat and fully channel my inner passive aggression

And I am not smart
Well, maybe sometimes I am
But golly, do I lack common sense
I also never understand sexual innuendos
I am so utterly scatter-brained at times, it's surprising to many, including myself, that I can even make it through the day

I don't have amazing friends
Well I do
But sometimes they're shitty too
Teasing me
Pointing out everything wrong with me
Shaming me for poor decisions
But sometimes they're the best
Celebrating my wins

Giving good advice
Helping me in my times of need
Making me laugh and smile and feel good

People are not amazed at my success and do not practically grovel at my feet
Well, at times they are and do
The compliments flow in
But so does the Imposter Syndrome
I feel like I'm deceiving them
They could sue me for false advertising based on their perceptions of me

And it's not easy to be like me
If anything, it's hard
The pressure I put on myself
The constant worry
The impossible goal of perfection
Ripping up paper
Screaming in angst
Picking myself apart

I'm also not super modest and open and honest and humble
I am and I'm not
I don't typically boast of modesty and humbleness
I don't fish for compliments nor do I flaunt my successes

But I don't hide them either
I feel a fair amount of pride when I do something well, but I'm selective with whom I share it
But I hide things too
I'm secretive
There are things I'm not open about
Few people know my deepest secrets
I sway the truth to make what I say more enticing
But it's my truth now
It is how I express myself
But I'm not a liar
When people raise their voice slightly, they're yelling in my world
When someone criticises me, they dislike me
It's just what my brain does, but it's my version of honesty
Subjectivity is my objectivity
But I try my best to be as upfront as possible without being overly assertive and too proud

I have so few talents
I'm so incredibly boring
I can't play sports
I can't roll my tongue
I can't get good grades without effort
I'm just average

I can't sing
Well I sort of can
I worked hard at it though
It didn't come naturally
Years of hard work did pay off, but I feel like
I'm cheating

I can't write
I love writing
But am I good at it?
I have good precision of my native language
I'm better at it than I am at speaking
When I write I'm at my most comfortable
But I don't fit in when I write
Creativity is good until conformity is necessary
My high school English grades can prove this
Maybe I can write well
But I can't write within the parameters of others
- only my own

I can't speak multiple languages
אני לא יכולה
Je peux pas
I like learning languages and I can communicate
in a few fairly well
But speaking them stresses me out
I get so nervous
What if I make a fool of myself?
What if I'm not understandable?

I can understand others fairly well, but speech
impediments and a lack of confidence cause
poor speech

My spelling skills? Not on point
I thought they were
Until Year 9 NAPLAN proved that my spelling
was one less than perfect when I didn't know
how to spell "resuscitate"
Clearly I am pretty ridiculous to think that my
spelling skills are useful
Although I am proud to say that I can spell
pneumonoultramicroscopicsilicovolcanoconiosis

I don't have great, big, different ideas, and if
people knew what was good for them, they
wouldn't agree with me
I'm too idealistic
I'm too romantic
I'm naïve
I'm too plain
I'm too basic
I'm too simple
No matter how many times I try to explain
myself, I get shut down in laughs
People appreciate my passion, but my
imagination isn't realistic enough for anyone
My utopia can only exist in a parallel universe
according to everyone else

Perfection can never be achieved, at least not in reality

But then I'm being too hard on myself, I'm told
But I don't want to be overly confident
I want the unattainable happy middle

Maybe I'm not perfect
Maybe I'm not flawless
Maybe nobody wants to be me
Maybe I don't get good grades
Maybe I'm not pretty
Maybe I'm not nice
Maybe I'm not smart
Maybe I don't have amazing friends
Maybe people are not amazed at my success and don't practically grovel at my feet
And maybe it's not easy to be like me
Maybe I'm also not super modest and open and honest and humble
Maybe I have so few talents
Maybe I can't sing
Maybe I can't write
Maybe I can't speak multiple languages
My spelling skills? Maybe they're not on point
Maybe I don't have great, big, different ideas, and if people knew what was good for them, they wouldn't agree with me
But I'm enough

# The Same in Any Age

Children are the same in any age
They cry when they're hungry
Or sad
Or scared
They notice the world around them
And internalise it
And interpret it
In their own unique way
Like drawing
Drawings of birds
Trees
Flowers
People
Bad things
Like guns
Or cages
Or Nazis
Because it's normal for kids to understand when they're hated
Because it should be normal for them to fear life or recognise who hates them
Because their drawings should feature them being stuck in a camp or their parents being murdered

Parents are the same in any age
They have the same desire to protect their children from harm
The same expectation to pass before their children
The same attempt to remain calm and strong in incredibly dire situations
The same responsibility to love their children no matter what
The same feelings when it doesn't go to plan

Bad people are the same in any age
The same blatantly disrespectful
The same nasty
The same criminal
The same murderous
They will never care

The same types of people are always the same -
In any age

# Tea

I was bored one night
I had nothing to do
I saw an interesting looking restaurant
I had heard various reviews about this place
I thought I'd give it a try

It seemed nice at first
The waiter had a friendly face
He complimented me
My cheeks went red
The attention was flattering

I make a mean tea, he said
Oh really? That's cool
Would you like to try it?

I was shocked
No waiter had ever offered me his tea before
Flattered at this unusual offer, I answered
Yeah, maybe
Great, I'll go prepare it

Then as he went to make it, I pondered to myself
Do I really want his tea?
He seems sweet enough
But I don't think I know him well enough for
him to make me his tea, let alone to try it

I don't want to seem rude
And he didn't pressure me into drinking it
But I don't want it anymore
I don't
I was just flattered and was trying to be polite

He came back to my table, tea in hand
Try it, he said
I'm really sorry, thank you for the offer, but I don't feel like it
But you said yes
I said maybe
Why? What changed?
I just thought about it and I don't want it anymore

JUST TRY IT

His face turned cold and evil
The anger in his eyes
It consumed me with fear

I said no

Too bad
He didn't care

I don't want it, you can't force me to have it

Well, I have you on camera
If you don't drink my tea

I'll expose how bad a customer you are
I'll broadcast it to the whole world
And no one will ever want to serve you again

I couldn't let that happen
I loved restaurants
I couldn't be banned from every single one
forever just for not trying his tea

Fine
I took a sip
Reluctantly
He smiled, he was very happy with my decision

Good, have some more
I don't want anymore
You have to or the whole world knows

I didn't want to agree
I really didn't want to
But I didn't want everyone to know what a bad customer I was
Reluctantly I drank some more
And some more
And some more
Please let me stop
No, I want you to try all my other tea

It's late
I don't want anymore

I don't care, this is my restaurant
Do as I say, bitch

So I stayed, gulping down cup after cup
Feeling devastatingly ill
Stomach moaning, feeling disheartened
I hated this tea
I hated this restaurant
I couldn't leave until he let me though

He didn't care about my feelings
It was only about his
He smiled, watching me drink the tea as though
he were watching a talent-filled performance
He became more and more excited
More and more eager
I wanted out
But he wouldn't listen
The threats kept coming

I told him he wasn't allowed to threaten me
He ignored me
All that mattered was that I drank his tea
Not even enjoyed it
Drank it
Pretended it was good
Even though it was pretty feral

I was there for hours
My reaction unchanged
He wanted something bigger

Better
My reaction wasn't enough for him
And then he left
He left me in the dark, deserted restaurant
As though *I* were disposable
As though *I* were the disappointment in this experience
Even though *he* was the one who forced me to drink his tea
Even though *he* was the one who gave me no choice
And then he just left me there as though I didn't just do him his favours

Is this what all waiters are like?
Is this what all customers eventually go through?
This restaurant is huge, many customers waiting to be served
Many waiters eager to serve innocent, unsuspecting customers
Hopefully, they're prepared
Because I wasn't

# Why She Writes

She writes to be heard
Her voice isn't loud enough
It's ignored
But her writing resounds
People pay attention
People listen
People connect
She isn't just a mere shadow in the background
But a triumphant noise that people hear as
impressive

She writes to be honest
To be expressive
She writes to not need to hide away behind fear
Her writing is her confidence
It's her personality
She is sassy
She is blunt
She is sarcastic
She's herself
When she writes her façade vanishes and she is
seen for who she truly is
Even if it's behind pen and paper

She writes to be coherent and concise
People can't understand her nervous thoughts
spilling out of her mouth
When she writes she is organised and sensible
She is intelligent
She just gets it
And people get her

She writes to prove a point
To others
To herself
To everyone
She writes to show she does have a voice
An opinion
She writes because she knows she can
To demonstrate her capabilities
Her hidden talents
That may have been invisible to others
previously

She writes to escape
To get away from the surrounding atrocities
To pretend she's somewhere else
Happy
Safe
Better

She writes to ignore the depressing reality
around her
She writes to be in a place where no one else can
bother her

She writes to pretend
To pretend her life is different
To pretend that she is someone else
To pretend that she is someone she's not
Someone brave
Someone confident
Someone outspoken
When in reality she is shy and timid and
thoughtless
She is quick-tempered and emotional and not
subtle
She is clumsy, she is stubborn, she is naïve

Or so her writing says
She writes to hide who she really is
Which no one will ever really know

www.ingramcontent.com/pod-product-compliance
Lightning Source LLC
Chambersburg PA
CBHW062145160726
48282CB00027B/944
* 9 7 8 9 3 5 7 6 1 9 9 6 7 *